THE REWARD OF PRAYER

And this is the confidence that we have in him, that, if we ask any thing according to his will, he heareth us.

1 John 5:14

....And that he is a rewarder of them that diligently seek him.

Hebrews 11:6

by
Franklin N. Abazie

The Reward of Prayer
COPYRIGHT 2016 BY Franklin N Abazie
ISBN: 978-1-94513301-5

All right reserved. This book or any portion thereof may not be reproduced or used in any manner whatsoever without the express written permission of the publisher, except for the use of brief quotations in a book review. All Bible quotes are from King James Version and others as noted.

Published by: F N ABAZIE PUBLISHING HOUSE—aka, Empowerment Bookstore

That I may publish with the voice of thanksgiving and tell of all thy wondrous works.
Psalms 26:7

To order additional copies, wholesales or booking call:
the Church office (973-372-7518)
or Empowerment Bookstore Hotline (973-393-8518)

Worship address:
343 Sanford Avenue, Newark, New Jersey 07106
Administrative Head Office address:
33 Schley Street Newark New Jersey 07112
Email: pastorfranknto@yahoo.com
Website www.fnabaziehealingministries.org
Publishing House: www.fnabaziepublishinghouse.org

This book is a production of F N Abazie Publishing House. A publication Arms of Miracle of God Ministries 2016.
First Edition

CONTENTS

THE MANDATE OF THE COMMISSION.....................iv
ARMS OF THE COMMISSION..v
INTRODUCTION...vi

CHAPTER 1
The Dynamics of Prayer...1

CHAPTER 2
The Help of the Holy Spirit....................................21

CHAPTER 3
The Benefits of Prayers...30

CHAPTER 4
Prayer of Salvation..49

CHAPTER 5
About the Author...73

THE MANDATE OF THE COMMISSION

"The moment is due to impact your world through the revival of the healing & miracle ministry of Jesus Christ of Nazareth.

"I am sending you to restore health unto thee and I will heal thee of thy wounds, said the Lord of Host."

ARMS OF THE COMMISSION

1) F N Abazie Ministries—Miracle of God Ministries (Miracle Chapel Intl)

2) F N Abazie TV Ministries: Global Television Ministry Outreach

3) F N Abazie Radio Ministries: Radio Broadcasting Outreach

4) F N Abazie Publishing House: Book Publication

5) F N Abazie Bible School: also called Word of Healing Bible School (W.O.H.B.S.)

6) F N Abazie Evangelistic Ass: Miracle of God Ministries: Global Crusade

7) Empowerment Bookstore: Book distribution

8) F N Abazie Helping Hands: Meeting the Help of the Needy Worldwide

9) F N Abazie Disaster Recovery Mission: Global Disaster Recovery

10) F N Abazie Prison Ministry: Prison Ministry For All Convicts "Second Chance"

Some of our ministry arms are awaiting the appointed time to commence.

INTRODUCTION

There's been so much ABUSE and NEGLECT concerning PRAYERS that we can no longer be quiet any more on this subject. In this book, you will appreciate THE REWARD OF PRAYERS into our lives.

> *And when thou prayest, thou shalt not be as the hypocrites are: for they love to pray standing in the synagogues and in the corners of the streets, that they may be seen of men. Verily I say unto you, They have their reward. But thou, when thou prayest, enter into thy closet, and when thou hast shut thy door, pray to thy Father which is in secret; and thy Father which seeth in secret shall reward thee openly. But when ye pray, use not vain repetitions, as the heathen do: for they think that they shall be heard for their much speaking. Be not ye therefore like unto them: for your Father knoweth what things ye have need of, before ye ask him.*
> **Matthew 6:5-8**

Prayer is a two-way communication channel. It is an avenue to talk to GOD with attention, humility, reverence, love and respect. *"GOD is a rewarder of those who deligently seek him."* (Hebrews 11:6)

The heartfelt and persistent prayer of a righteous man (believer) can accomplish much when put into action and made effective by God—it is dynamic and can have tremendous power. (See James 5:17.) That is my introduction in a nutshell.

HIGHLIGHTS

HOW TO PRAY PREVAILING PRAYERS

REPENT

REPENTANCE is a primary prerequisite that is of utmost importance on the subject of PRAYERS. The first step into HEALING is "REPENTANCE." The HOLY SPIRIT intervention is quick and swift only when GOD sees a humble REPENTED HEART. Peter replied to a question from the crowd "what shall we do?" with the following reply: *"Repent and be baptized every one of you, in the name of Jesus Christ for the forgiveness of your sins. And you will receive the gift of the Holy Spirit."* (Acts 2:38) Every time we truly REPENT, GOD genuinely RESTORES OUR LIVES. *"Therefore say thou unto them, Thus saith the Lord of hosts; Turn ye unto me, saith the Lord of hosts, and I will turn unto you, saith the Lord of hosts."* (Zechariah 1:3)

FAITH

*But without faith it is impossible to please him:
for he that cometh to God must believe that he is,
and that he is a rewarder of them
that diligently seek him.*
Hebrews 11:6

Unless otherwise stated, THE PRAYER OF FAITH will not save the sick unless the MYSTERY

OF FAITH is deeply invoked. *"And the prayer of faith shall save the sick."* (James 5:15) It took the mystery of faith for the Bible to say, *"The effectual fervent prayer of a righteous man availeth much."* (James 5:16) WE ARE ADMONISHED IN THE SCRIPTURES—

But ye beloved, building up your selves on your most holy faith, praying in the Holy Ghost.
Jude 1:20

The mystery of Faith is a primary prerequisite for all prayers to be victorious. We must therefore develop supernatural faith—especially in prayer. My book, *The Supernatural Power of Faith*, will be of great help to you.

DECISION

Decisions are the wheels of destiny. Decisions are like horses which we ride into FAME—or into SHAME. Until we repent and accept Jesus Christ as our Lord and savior, we are not ready to receive the Holy Spirit. Decisions are the pillars to determine the outcome of our lives. Most of the events of our lifetime were all directly proportional to our decisions

Decisions are the building blocks into the success of our future. For example, whenever we settle for low-paying jobs, we are entitled to the lower wages and low salaries. Lazarus settled to eat crumbs. *"And there was a certain beggar named Lazarus, which was laid at his gate, full of sores, And desiring to be fed with the crumbs which fell from the rich man's table: moreover the dogs came and licked his sores."* (Luke 16:20-21) Despite all the wealth of the father, the prodigal son decided to eat the pig's food.

THE DECISION OF THE PRODIGAL SON

And he said, A certain man had two sons: And the younger of them said to his father, Father, give me the portion of goods that falleth to me. And he divided unto them his living. And not many days after the younger son gathered all together, and took his journey into a far country, and there wasted his substance with riotous living. And when he had spent all, there arose a mighty famine in that land; and he began to be in want. And he went and joined himself to a citizen of that country; and he sent him into his fields to feed swine. And he would fain have filled his belly with the husks that the swine did eat: and no man gave unto him. And when he came to himself, he said, How many hired servants of my father's have bread enough and to spare, and I perish with hunger! I will arise and go to my father, and will say unto him, Father, I have sinned against heaven, and before thee, And am no more worthy to be called thy son: make me as one of thy hired servants. And he arose, and came to his father. But when he was yet a great way off, his father saw him, and had compassion, and ran, and fell on his neck, and kissed him. And the son said unto him, Father, I have sinned against heaven, and in thy sight, and am no more worthy to be called thy

son. But the father said to his servants, Bring forth the best robe, and put it on him; and put a ring on his hand, and shoes on his feet: And bring hither the fatted calf, and kill it; and let us eat, and be merry: For this my son was dead, and is alive again; he was lost, and is found. And they began to be merry.
Luke 15:14-22

PRAYER

But ye beloved, building up your selves on your most holy faith, praying in the Holy Ghost.
Jude 1:20

PRAYING in the SPIRIT permits us to experience the anointing of GOD. Every time we pray feverently IN THE SPIRIT, WE ENCOUNTER THE PRESENCE OF THE HOLY SPIRIT. The Bible says likewise the Spirit also helpeth our infirmities; for we know not what we should pray for as we ought: but the Spirit itself maketh intercession for us with groaning which cannot be uttered. EVERY TIME we pray in tongue (PRAYING IN THE SPIRIT), we provoke the presence of the HOLY GHOST. Most of the relief and assurance that will come into your life is only possible with the assistance of the Holy Spirit.

PRAYER POINTS TO ACTIVATE THE PRESENCE OF THE HOLY SPIRIT

1) Holy Spirit, reveal yourself to me, in the Name of Jesus.

2) Holy Spirit, crush every daily habit of sin, in the Name of Jesus.

3) Holy Spirit, become my companion today, in the Name of Jesus.

4) Holy Spirit, grant me access, in the Name of Jesus.

5) Power of God, grant me the GRACE to live right for Jesus Christ.

6) Hand of God, deliver me from sin, in the Name of Jesus.

7) Fire of God, burn every sinful thoughts from my mind, in the Name of Jesus.

8) I proclaim authority over every prevailing sin in my life, in Jesus Name.

9) I destroy every root of sin in my life, in Jesus Name.

10) Sin shall not have dominion over my life, in the Name of Jesus.

11) Lord God, emphasize genuine repentance over my spirit man, in the Name of Jesus

12) Holy Spirit, revive and rekindle your fire of revival inside of me, in the Name of Jesus.

13) Power of God, hijack the controlling forces oppressing my life, in the Name of Jesus.

14) Blood of Jesus, take over my life, in the Name of Jesus.

15) O Lord, baptize me with the gift of the Holy Spirit.

16) Holy Spirit, breathe afresh upon my life, in the Name of Jesus.

17) Holy Spirit, take possession of my will, in the Name of Jesus.

18) Holy Spirit, make yourself real to me, in the name of Jesus.

19) Holy Spirit, fan your revival fire upon my life, in the name of Jesus.

THE MYSTERIES & DYNAMICS OF PRAYERS

Epaphras, who is one of you, a servant of Christ, saluteth you, always labouring fervently for you in prayers that ye may stand perfect and complete in all the will of God.
Colossians 4:12

Although there are some prevailing arguments about FAITH by some unbelievers, genuine PRAYERS produce DIVINE INTERVENTION. We will never be victorious in the race of life until we labor in PRAYERS. PRAYER is labor. You will agree with me that labor is no cheap talk. I read a testimony of one great man of GOD who increased his prayer lifestyle from three hours daily to five to eight hours daily.

The divine assigned place to receive the access code of victory is at the place of PRAYERS.

Jesus prayed until the fashion of HIS countenance was altered. And as he prayed, the fashion of his countenance was altered, and his raiment was white and glistering.
Luke 9:29

PRAYER is the meeting point between DIVINITY and HUMANITY. John Wesley, founder of the Methodist church, once said that "it appears like GOD will do nothing, until somebody prays." Prayer is so vital that it grants hope, assurance, courage and peace of mind to any prevailing circumstances.

FEW HIGH POINTS:

We must pray from the a genuine repented heart.

We must pray with a pure conscience.

We must pray kingdom prayers—"thy kingdom come."

We must pray for one another.

We must pray with a love.

We must pray sincerely.

We must pray for the promotion of the kingdom of God.

We must pray for our pastor and elders in the church.

We must prayer for our leaders.

We must pray for our families.

We must pray for the sick.

We must pray for the church of Christ.

CHAPTER 1
THE DYNAMICS OF PRAYER

The heartfelt and persistent prayer of a righteous man (believer) can accomplish much [when put into action and made effective by God—it is dynamic and can have tremendous power.
James 5:16

WHAT IS PRAYER?

One of the strangest mysteries science has been unable to uncover is the DYNAMICS OF PRAYER. Oftentimes the scientist wonders how we can utter words into the atmosphere, only to see those words bring healing to someone who is sick. The connection and mysteries of prayer are linked to the ALMIGHTY GOD IN HEAVEN. If you can understand GOD in HIS infinite attributes, then you will comprehend the force and power of prayers to heal the sick, to raise the dead, to deliver the oppressed, to let go of the captive, to breakthrough someone in captivity and in poverty.

PRAYER means talking and listening directly to GOD with reverence, respect, attention and love. Prayer is the force of change. Prayer is the key to deliverance and triumphant in life. Prayer is the primary access to divine health.

Prayer is a mystery that is inexplicably dynamic, if we consider the mysteries of how it works. It has been INEVITABLE for medical science to write off PRAYERS at HOSPTIALS. Terminally sick patients are given the RIGHT to RECEIVE their LAST RITES and PRAYERS.

Among the Biblically-defined strategies and techniques to pray is to PRAY WITH UNDERSTANDING.

Let my prayer be set forth before thee as incense; and the lifting up of my hands as the evening sacrifice.
Psalms 141:2

For example, if we are PRAYING FOR A BREAKTHROUGH in life, then it requires asking for the FAVOR OF GOD. But if we are PRAYING FOR DELIVERANCE, we engage the hand of the LORD to SAVE US in PRAYERS. We skillfully go into a deeper dimension of warfare, pleading with the FATHER TO SEND ANGELIC ASSISTANCE. The archangel Michael is usually dispatched to come down in the REALMS OF THE SPIRIT TO ENGAGE THE ENEMY IN THE BATTLE.

Again, if we are PRAYING to inflict punishment upon the opposition, we ask for the VENGEANCE OF GOD. We are assured to provoke the vengeance of GOD when we PRAY/PRAISE through melodies and render victory songs unto GOD.

*Let the high praises of God be in their mouth,
and a two-edged sword in their hand;
To execute vengeance upon the heathen,
and punishments upon the people; To bind their kings
with chains, and their nobles with fetters of iron;
To execute upon them the judgment written:
this honour have all his saints. Praise ye the Lord.*
Psalms 149:6-9

GOD is obligated to REWARD us all, as long as we pray with the right perspective. *"But thou, when thou prayest, enter into thy closet, and when thou hast shut thy door, pray to thy Father which is in secret; and thy Father which seeth in secret shall reward thee openly."* (Matthew 6:6)

*...And that he is a rewarder of them
that diligently seek him.*
Hebrews 11:6

HOW DO WE PRAY?

But thou, when thou prayest, enter into thy closet, and when thou hast shut thy door, pray to thy Father which is in secret; and thy Father which seeth in secret shall reward thee openly. But when ye pray, use not vain repetitions, as the heathen do: for they think that they shall be heard for their much speaking.
Be not ye therefore like unto them: for your Father knoweth what things ye have need of, before ye ask him. After this manner therefore pray ye: Our Father which art in heaven, Hallowed be thy name. Thy kingdom come, Thy will be done in earth, as it is in heaven. Give us this day our daily bread. And forgive us our debts, as we forgive our debtors. And lead us not into temptation, but deliver us from evil: For thine is the kingdom, and the power, and the glory, for ever. Amen. For if ye forgive men their trespasses, your heavenly Father will also forgive you.
Matthew 6:6-14

HOW DO I PRAY?

We must humble ourselves in PRAYER with ATTENTION, REVERENCE & RESPECT to GOD.

We must humble our selves irrespective of our affluence in society or job position.

*If my people, which are called by my name,
shall humble themselves, and pray, and seek my face,
and turn from their wicked ways; then will I hear from
heaven, and will forgive their sin, and will heal their
land. Now mine eyes shall be open, and mine ears attent
unto the prayer that is made in this place.*
2 Chronicles 7:14-15

WE MUST RESPECT & HONOR THE PRESENCE OF THE ALMIGHTY GOD

Every time we despise the presence of GOD, we suffer the consequences.

*For them that honour me I will honour,
and they that despise me shall be lightly esteemed.*
1 Samuel 2:30

We are commanded by the scripture to HONOR GOD. If we are obedient to our earthly parents, how much more our HEAVENLY FATHER? *"Honour thy father and mother; which is the first commandment with promise."* (Ephesians 6:2)

We prove our sonship when we HONOR GOD IN PRAYERS.

*A son honoureth his father, and a servant his master:
if then I be a father, where is mine honour? and if I
be a master, where is my fear? saith the Lord of hosts
unto you, O priests, that despise my name. And ye say,
Wherein have we despised thy name?*
Malachi 1:6-9

WE MUST REVERENCE GOD IN PRAYERS

PRAYER IS A TWO-WAY COMMUNICATION BETWEEN US AND GOD. PRAYER means talking and listening directly to GOD with reverence, respect, attention and love. Although so many of us are selfish, we just want GOD to HEAR us out—we don't want to LISTEN to GOD talk back to us. Prayer is a two-way communication channel. Whenever we speak to GOD in PRAYER, we must create time to MEDIATE and LISTEN when GOD is talking back to us with RESPECT, LOVE, HUMILITY and REVRENCE. We must REVERENCE the name of God in Prayers, because it is HOLY.

*He sent redemption unto his people:
he hath commanded his covenant forever:
holy and reverend is his name.*
Psalms 111:9

Although we must RESPECT, REVERENCE and HUMBLE ourselves before GOD, if our heart is not right with Him, He will not hear us. *"Then shall they cry unto the Lord, but he will not hear them: he will even hide his face from them at that time, as they have behaved themselves ill in their doings."* (Micah 3:4)

As long as we live in sin and disobedience, GOD will not hear our prayers.

> *But your iniquities have separated between you and your God, and your sins have hid his face from you, that he will not hear.*
> **Isaiah 59:2**

"Therefore it is come to pass, that as he cried, and they would not hear; so they cried, and I would not hear, saith the Lord of hosts." (Zechariah 7:13) Prayers must be done CORRECTLY for you to RECEIVE speedy INTERVENTION.

WHAT IS THE RIGHT WAY TO PRAY UNTO GOD?

Our typical example on how to PRAY is the prayer Jesus taught his disciples to pray in Luke11:1-4. *"And it came to pass, that, as he was praying in a certain place, when he ceased, one of his disciples said unto him, Lord, teach us to pray, as John also taught his disciples. And he said unto them, When ye pray, say, Our Father which art in heaven, Hallowed be thy name. Thy kingdom come. Thy will be done, as in heaven, so in earth. Give us day by day our daily bread. And forgive us our sins; for we also forgive every one that is indebted to us. And lead us not into temptation; but deliver us from evil."* (Luke 11:1-4)

RESPECT
...Say, *Our Father which art in heaven...*

REVERENCE
...Hallowed be thy name. Thy kingdom come...

HONOR
...Thy will be done, as in heaven, so in Earth...

REQUEST
...Give us day by day our daily bread. And forgive us our sins; for we also forgive every one that is indebted to us. And lead us not into temptation; but deliver us from evil.

The Holy Scripture attested that GOD does not hear sinners, but if any man worships HIM and does HIS will, GOD is COVENANTLY OBLIGATED to INTERVENE.

> *Now we know that God heareth not sinners: but if any man be a worshipper of God, and doeth his will, him he heareth.*
> **John 9:31**

WHO IS A SINNER?

Everyone operating outside of the commandment of the scripture is a sinner in my opinion. Whenever you disobey God, reject God, mock God, ignorantly neglect the presence and sovereignty of God, you are a sinner.

He that committeth sin is of the devil;
for the devil sinneth from the beginning;
For this purpose the son of God was manifested
that he might destroy the works of the devil.
1 John 3:8

It is easy to lie and hide from a man, but very difficult to hide from the PRESENCE OF GOD. For God does not look like man. *"For my thoughts are not your thoughts, neither are your ways my ways, saith the Lord. For as the heavens are higher than the earth, so are my ways higher than your ways, and my thoughts than your thoughts."* (Isaiah 55:8-9)

For the Lord seeth not as man seeth;
for man looketh on the outward appearance,
but the Lord looketh on the heart.
1 Samuel 16:9

Remember...

David could not run away from THE PRESENCE OF GOD. David said, *"Whither shall I go from thy spirit? or whither shall I flee from thy presence? If I ascend up into heaven, thou art there: if I make my bed in hell, behold, thou art there. If I take the wings of the morning, and dwell in the uttermost parts of the sea; Even there shall thy hand lead me, and thy right hand shall hold me."* (Psalms 139:7-10)

He that covereth his sins shall not prosper: but whoso confesseth and forsaketh them shall have mercy.
Proverbs 28:13

We live in a time where there is so much SINFUL advertisement hitting us at every street corner—from the newspapers to the television—we are bombarded daily with immoral images, ALCOHOL ads and SINFULLY LUSTFUL appeals from the TV. As confusing as sin can interpreted in these evil times, it is extremely difficult for church folks to tell the difference between what is sinful and what is righteous. *"He that doeth righteousness is righteous, even as he is righteous."* (1 John 3:7)

Unless otherwise stated, all who live in disobedience of the commandment of GOD are doomed to be called SINNERS. Everyone living an unethical and immoral lifestyle, everyone living in an unrighteous lifestyle, is a sinner. We are admonished—*"Love not the world, neither the things that are in the world. If any man love the world, the love of the Father is not in him. For all that is in the world, the lust of the flesh, and the lust of the eyes, and the pride of life, is not of the Father, but is of the world."* (1 John 2:15-16)

James 4:1-5 emphasized a profound statement about living in sin: *"From whence come wars and fightings among you? come they not hence, even of your lusts that war in your members? Ye lust, and have not: ye kill, and desire to have, and cannot obtain: ye fight and war, yet ye have not, because ye ask not. Ye ask, and receive not, because ye ask amiss, that ye may consume it upon your lusts. Ye adulterers and adulteresses, know ye not that the friendship of the world is enmity with God? whosoever therefore will be a friend of the world is the enemy of God. Do ye think that the scripture saith in vain, The spirit that dwelleth in us lusteth to envy?"*

Examine yourselves, whether ye be in the faith; prove your own selves. Know ye not your own selves, how that Jesus Christ is in you, except ye be reprobates?
2 Corinthians 13:5

The Holy Bible defined SIN from RIGHTEOUSNESS in a clear and precise term that cannot be mistaken. Despite our IGNORANCE, some of us still MISREPRESENT and MISINTERPRET the scripture. We tend to JUSTIFY our SINFUL actions with our own INTERPRETATION of the SCRIPTURE. From my small understanding, everyone operating within the scope of Galatians 5:20-21 is classified as a sinner.

Now the works of the flesh are manifest, which are these; Adultery, fornication, uncleanness, lasciviousness, Idolatry, witchcraft, hatred, variance, emulations, wrath, strife, seditions, heresies, Envyings, murders, drunkenness, revellings, and such like: of the which I tell you before, as I have also told you in time past, that they which do such things shall not inherit the kingdom of God.
Galatians 5:20-21

Further supporting scripture...

But the fearful, and unbelieving, and the abominable, and murderers, and whoremongers, and sorcerers, and idolaters, and all liars, shall have their part in the lake which burneth with fire and brimstone: which is the second death.
Revelation 21:8

WHO, THEREFORE, IS A SINNER?

1) The Lazy Man: There are a lot of church folks who uses PRAYER and FASTING as an excuse as to why they should not do productive work. It is sinful for any able body man/woman to fold their hand and make themselves beggars before man and the Spirit of GOD.

The Bible says, *"the sluggard will not plow by reason of the cold; therefore shall he beg in harvest, and have nothing."* (Proverbs 20:4) In my understanding, laziness is a sin. *"For even when we were with you, this we commanded you, that if any would not work, neither should he eat."* (2 Thessalonians 3:10)

Covenant mentality demands that we all understand that God has done His part over our lives. Jesus said I must work. It is dignified for every believer to earn money through the work of their hands. *"The sleep of a labouring man is sweet, whether he eat little or much."* (Ecclesiastes 5:12)

Although most lazy people live in denial and tend to blame someone else, nevertheless, Godliness demands that we take absolute responsibility for the outcome of our lives.

2) Unbelievers: In my view, all that have not acknowledged Jesus Christ as Lord and savior are sinners. The Bible says *God heareth not sinners.* Without contradiction, all unbelievers live in a sinful lifestyle. Unless God has mercy, most unbelievers will not make eternity in heaven.

HOW DO I COME OUT OF SIN?

These prevailing dominating controlling forces will not casually go away. Unless you're taking actions by faith, those evil forces will continue to remote control your life and destiny.

You must **REPENT** and **CONFESS and PROCLAIM** THE LORD JESUS CHRIST. *"The word says as many as received him, to them gave He power to become the sons of God. Even to them that believe on his name."* (John 1:12)

To qualify for divine visitation, do the following (with sincerity):

1) *Acknowledge* that you are a sinner and that He died for you. (Romans 3:23)

2) *Repent of your sins.* (Acts 3:19, Luke 13:5, 2 Peter 3:9)

3) ***Believe in your heart*** that Jesus died for your sin. (Romans 10:10)

4) ***Confess Jesus as the Lord over your life.*** (Romans 10:10, Acts 2:21)

Now repeat this Prayer after me—

Say Lord Jesus, I accept you today, as my Lord and my savior, forgive me of my sins wash me with your blood. Right now, I believe, I am sanctified, I am save, I am free, I am free from the Power of sin to serve the Lord Jesus. Thank you Lord for saving me. Amen.

Congratulations.

YOU ARE NOW A BORN AGAIN CHRISTIAN!

WHEN & HOW OFTEN SHOULD WE PRAY?

ALWAYS

Although there are never enough PRAYERS, we are commanded by the Holy Bible to PRAY ALWAYS.

Praying always with all prayer and supplication in the Spirit, and watching thereunto with all perseverance and supplication for all saints.
Ephesians 6:18

*I thank my God upon every remembrance of you,
Always in every prayer of mine for you all
making request with joy.*
Philippians 1:3-4

We must PRAY ALWAYS. *"We give thanks to God and the Father of our Lord Jesus Christ, praying always for you."* (Colossians 1:3) Oftentimes most of us PRAY AND BACKSLIDE. We are commanded to PRAY without CEASING. *"Pray without ceasing."* (1 Thessalonians 5:17) We miss our opportunity and our due season when we PRAY AND FAINT. *"And let us not be weary in well doing: for in due season we shall reap, if we faint not."* (Galatians 6:9)

How Should We Pray?

WE MUST PRAY IN THE SPIRIT

Satan does not understand the language of the **Spirit**. Every time we **pray in the spirit** we confuse and defeat the devil with the language of the angels. "For if I pray in an unknown tongue, my spirit prayeth, but my understanding is unfruitful. What is it then? I will pray with the spirit, and I will pray with the understanding also: I will sing with the spirit, and I will sing with the understanding also." (1 Corinthians 14:14-15)

WE MUST PRAY SINCERELY FROM A GENUINE CONSCIENCE

Remember Hanna, for example

"And she was in bitterness of soul, and prayed unto the Lord, and wept sore. And she vowed a vow, and said, O Lord of hosts, if thou wilt indeed look on the affliction of thine handmaid, and remember me, and not forget thine handmaid, but wilt give unto thine handmaid a man child, then I will give him unto the Lord all the days of his life, and there shall no razor come upon his head. And it came to pass, as she continued praying before the Lord, that Eli marked her mouth." (1 samuel 1:10-12)

Remember Hezekiah as a second example

"In those days was Hezekiah sick unto death. And Isaiah the prophet the son of Amoz came unto him, and said unto him, Thus saith the Lord, Set thine house in order: for thou shalt die, and not live. Then Hezekiah turned his face toward the wall, and prayed unto the Lord, And said, Remember now, O Lord, I beseech thee, how I have walked before thee in truth and with a perfect heart, and have done that which is good in thy sight. And Hezekiah wept sore." (Isaiah 38:1-3)

"Then Jonah prayed unto the Lord his God out of the fish's belly, And said, I cried by reason of mine affliction unto the Lord, and he heard me; out of the belly of hell cried I, and thou heardest my voice." (Jonah 2:1-2)

WE MUST PRAY FROM A THANKSGIVING, CHEERFUL HEART

If we must **pray** and get **rewarded**, we must enter into **His presence** with thanksgiving—not with **murmuring and complaining**. Never come to the place of prayer with anger, bitterness and sadness. *"Enter into his gates with thanksgiving, and into his courts with praise: be thankful unto him, and bless his name."* (Psalms 100:4)

WE MUST PRAY WITH FAITH

Like I stated earlier, the prayer of faith will not save the sick unless there is **faith in such prayer**. *"But let him ask in faith, with no doubting, for the one who doubts is like a wave of the sea that is driven and tossed by the wind."* (James 1:6)

What Should We Pray For?

WE MUST PRAY KINGDOM ORIENTED PRAYERS

We shall never prevail in prayers unless we focus on the kingdom of God. *"But seek ye first the kingdom of God, and his righteousness; and all these things shall be added unto you."* (Matthew 6:33) *"And he said unto them, When ye pray, say, Our Father which art in heaven, Hallowed be thy name. Thy kingdom come. Thy will be done, as in heaven, so in earth."* (Luke 11:1-2)

One of my great mentors, Archbishop Benson Idahosa, used to say it this way: "Go after the commission in prayers and the commission will bring the addition in our lives."

SUMMARY OF CHAPTER ONE

Prayer is a two-way communication dialogue. It is a serene meeting place with God, where **divinity** meets with **humanity**. Dynamic prayers require that we understand the **right way to pray to God**.

And it came to pass, that, as he was praying in a certain place, when he ceased, one of his disciples said unto him, Lord, teach us to pray, as John also taught his disciples. And he said unto them, When ye pray, say, Our Father which art in heaven, Hallowed be thy name. Thy kingdom come. Thy will be done, as in heaven, so in earth. Give us day by day our daily bread. And forgive us our sins; for we also forgive every one that is indebted to us. And lead us not into temptation; but deliver us from evil.
Luke 11:1-4

WE MUST RESPECT GOD IN PRAYER
...say, Our Father which art in heaven...

WE MUST REVERENCE GOD IN PRAYER
...Hallowed be thy name. Thy kingdom come...

WE MUST HONOR GOD IN PRAYER
...Thy will be done, as in heaven, so in earth...

WE MUST MAKE OUR SUPPLICATION KNOWN TO GOD IN PRAYERS

...Give us day by day our daily bread. And forgive us our sins; for we also forgive every one that is indebted to us. And lead us not into temptation; but deliver us from evil.

Remember...God does not hear sinners. *"Now we know that God heareth not sinners: but if any man be a worshipper of God, and doeth his will, him he heareth."* (John 9:31)

The keys to divine health are released by God on the platform of the power and dynamics of prayer.

I must tell you this and it must be here— ***prayer works.*** I am a living testimony of the handiwork of prayer. I admonish you, therefore, to begin a **prayer lifestyle**. The people that **pray** do not develop mental disease. The people that **pray** do not die untimely deaths. As long as you **pray,** there is help on the way.

Remember...

The potency and power of prayer is released on the platform of the covenant.

CHAPTER 2
THE HELP OF THE HOLY SPIRIT

In this evil dispensation that we live in, we are doomed without the help of the HOLY SPIRIT.

But ye, beloved, building up yourselves on your most holy faith, praying in the Holy Ghost.
Jude 1:20

We must totally depend on the HOLY SPIRIT IN OUR PRAYERS.

Likewise the Spirit also helpeth our infirmities: for we know not what we should pray for as we ought: but the Spirit itself maketh intercession for us with groanings which cannot be uttered.
Romans 8:26

THE HELP OF THE HOLY SPIRIT IN OUR PRAYERS

FELLOWSHIP

We cannot genuinely have fellowship with the Almighty GOD without the intervention of the HOLY SPIRIT. *"But if we walk in the light, as he is in the light, we have fellowship one with another, and the blood of Jesus Christ his Son cleanseth us from all sin."* (1 John 1:7) Our prayer life will be frustrated as long as we do not commune with the HOLY SPIRIT.

CORRECTION & REPROOFS

Every time we sin it is the POLICEMAN of the heart—a.k.a. our CONSCIENCE—through the help of the HOLY SPIRIT, that pricks and troubles OUR HEART. *"I say the truth in Christ, I lie not, my conscience also bearing me witness in the Holy Ghost."* (Romans 9:1) Most of us with a strong stone heart will never REPENT unless the HOLY SPIRIT intervenes. *"Turn you at my reproof: behold, I will pour out my spirit unto you, I will make known my words unto you."* (Proverbs 1:23)

INSTRUCTOR

Our only instructor in PRAYERS is the person of the HOLY SPIRIT. The Bible says, *"Likewise the Spirit also helpeth our infirmities: for we know not what we should pray for as we ought: but the Spirit itself maketh intercession for us with groanings which cannot be uttered."* (Romans 8:26)

For all our prayers to be answered, we must depend on the help of the HOLY SPIRIT IN OUR PRAYERS. *"I will instruct thee and teach thee in the way which thou shalt go: I will guide thee with mine eye."* (Psalms 32:8) It is written: *"Thou gavest also thy good spirit to instruct them, and withheldest not thy manna from their mouth, and gavest them water for their thirst."* (Nehemiah 9:20)

CONVICTS US

All my grammar will do nothing to you unless the HOLY SPIRIT intervenes. *"Nevertheless I tell you the truth; It is expedient for you that I go away: for if I go not away, the Comforter will not come unto you; but if I depart, I will send him unto you. And when he is come, he will reprove the world of sin, and of righteousness, and of judgment: Of sin, because they believe not on me; Of righteousness, because I go to my Father, and ye see me no more; Of judgment, because the prince of this world is judged."* (John 16:7-11)

THE ONLY PERSON WHO CAN GENUINELY CAUSE US TO REPENT IS THE HOLY SPIRIT. Genuine repentance and conviction is possible with the help of the Holy Spirit. *"Now when they heard this, they were pricked in their heart, and said unto Peter and to the rest of the apostles, Men and brethren, what shall we do? Then Peter said unto them, Repent, and be baptized every one of you in the name of Jesus Christ for the remission of sins, and ye shall receive the gift of the Holy Ghost."* (Acts 2:37-38)

THE HOLY SPIRIT IS
THE UNQUENCHABLE FIRE

"I indeed baptize you with water unto repentance. but he that cometh after me is mightier than I, whose shoes I am not worthy to bear: he shall baptize you with the Holy Ghost, and with fire: Whose fan is in his hand, and he will throughly purge his floor, and gather his wheat into the garner; but he will burn up the chaff with unquenchable fire." (Matthew 3:11-12) No matter how much PRAYERS

ARE OFFERED UNTO GOD IN THE CHURCH, there will be no REVIVAL IN THE CHURCH OF GOD without the help of the Holy Spirit.

THE HOLY SPIRIT IS THE REFINER'S FIRE

Behold, I will send my messenger, and he shall prepare the way before me: and the Lord, whom ye seek, shall suddenly come to his temple, even the messenger of the covenant, whom ye delight in: behold, he shall come, saith the Lord of hosts. But who may abide the day of his coming? and who shall stand when he appeareth? for he is like a refiner's fire, and like fullers' soap: And he shall sit as a refiner and purifier of silver: and he shall purify the sons of Levi, and purge them as gold and silver, that they may offer unto the Lord an offering in righteousness.
Malachi 3:1-3

HOW TO ACTIVATE THE HOLY SPIRIT IN PRAYERS

PURIFICATION

TO ACTIVATE THE HOLY SPIRIT, WE MUST MAINTAIN A PURE AND SANCTIFIED LIFESTYLE. We will never be used by GOD unless we clean, repent and embrace righteousness. *"If a man therefore purge himself from these, he shall be a vessel unto honour, sanctified, and meet for the master's use, and prepared unto every good work."* (2 Timothy 2:21) *"...A broken and a contrite heart, O God, thou wilt not despise."* (Psalms 51:17)

EMPOWERMENT

Unless the HOLY SPIRIT HELPS US, we will not be able to speak with POWER and AUTHORITY. The apostles gained BOLDNESS and AUTHORITY WHEN the Holy Spirit appeared in the first church. The Bible says how God anointed Jesus of Nazareth with the HOLY GHOST and with POWER, who went about doing good and healing all that were oppressed of the devil, for God was with him. *"...And there appeared unto them cloven tongues like as of fire, and it sat upon each of them. And they were all filled with the Holy Ghost, and began to speak with other tongues, as the Spirit gave them utterance."* (Acts 2:4)

CONDITIONS TO RECEIVE THE HOLY SPIRIT

REPENTANCE

Unless we repent, the Holy Spirit will leave us alone. *"Repent, and be baptized every one of you in the name of Jesus Christ for the remission of sins, and ye shall receive the gift of the Holy Ghost."* (Acts 2:38)

BE BAPTIZED

"...be baptized every one of you in the name of Jesus Christ for the remission of sins, and ye shall receive the gift of the Holy Ghost." (Acts 2:38)

CONFESS OF YOUR SIN
"If we confess our sins, he is faithful and just to forgive us our sins, and to cleanse us from all unrighteousness." (1 John 1:9)

ACKNOWLEDGMENT
"Acknowledge that you are a sinner and that Jesus Christ died for your sins." (Romans 3:23)

BORN AGAIN
WE MUST BE BORN AGAIN!

How do you get born again?

For with the heart man believeth unto righteousness; and with the mouth confession is made unto salvation.
Romans 10:10

Remember.....

*Jesus answered and said unto him, Verily, verily,
I say unto thee, Except a man be born again, he cannot
see the kingdom of God. Nicodemus saith unto him, How
can a man be born when he is old? can he enter
the second time into his mother's womb, and be born?
Jesus answered, Verily, verily, I say unto thee,
Except a man be born of water and of the Spirit,
he cannot enter into the kingdom of God. That which is
born of the flesh is flesh; and that which is born of the
Spirit is spirit. Marvel not that I said unto thee,
Ye must be born again. The wind bloweth where it
listeth, and thou hearest the sound thereof, but canst
not tell whence it cometh, and whither it goeth:
so is every one that is born of the Spirit.*
John 3:3-8

CONDITION TO ANSWERED PRAYERS

REPENTANCE

"Repent, and be baptized every one of you in the name of Jesus Christ for the remission of sins, and ye shall receive the gift of the Holy Ghost." (Acts 2:38)

BE BAPTIZED

"....be baptized every one of you in the name of Jesus Christ for the remission of sins, and ye shall receive the gift of the Holy Ghost." (Acts 2:38)

CONFESS OF YOUR SIN
"If we confess our sins, he is faithful and just to forgive us our sins, and to cleanse us from all unrighteousness." (1 John 1:9)

ACKNOWLEDGMENT
"Acknowledge that you are a sinner and that Jesus Christ died for your sins." (Romans 3:23)

BORN AGAIN
For our prayers to be answered, we must be born again. *"Jesus answered and said unto him, Verily, verily, I say unto thee, Except a man be born again, he cannot see the kingdom of God. Nicodemus saith unto him, How can a man be born when he is old? can he enter the second time into his mother's womb, and be born? Jesus answered, Verily, verily, I say unto thee, Except a man be born of water and of the Spirit, he cannot enter into the kingdom of God. That which is born of the flesh is flesh; and that which is born of the Spirit is spirit. Marvel not that I said unto thee, Ye must be born again. The wind bloweth where it listeth, and thou hearest the sound thereof, but canst not tell whence it cometh, and whither it goeth: so is every one that is born of the Spirit."* (John 3:3-8)

ASK IN FAITH
Every time we ask and we do not get answers, it is because we are not asking in faith. If we ask in faith in prayers, GOD is obligated to intervene on our behalf. It is written: *"Ye ask, and receive not, because ye*

ask amiss, that ye may consume it upon your lusts." (James 4:3) I DARE YOU, ASK IN FAITH AND SEE HOW GOD WILL RESPOND SPEEDILY. *"Until now you have not asked for anything in my name. Ask and you will receive, and your joy will be complete."* (John 16:24/NIV)

CHAPTER 3
THE BENEFITS OF PRAYERS

Let my prayer be set forth before thee as incense; and the lifting up of my hands as the evening sacrifice.
Psalms 141:2

PRAYER is our only link to communicate with our HEAVENLY FATHER. It is the believer's lifeline. Although PRAYER has been grossly neglected in public school, prayer is the only platform for raising Godly children and future generations. A recent Pew Research Poll in 2013 showed that over half of Americans pray every day. Let's briefly examine some undeniable benefits of prayers.

1) PRAYER GRANTS CONFIDENCE & ASSURANCE

And this is the confidence that we have in him, that, if we ask any thing according to his will, he heareth us: And if we know that he hear us, whatsoever we ask, we know that we have the petitions that we desired of him.
1 John 5:14-15

So many people without a PRAYER LIFE lose CONFIDENCE and SELF-ASSURANCE, oftentimes committing SUICIDE. A genuine PRAYER LIFE grants long life, confidence and assurance in

GOD. With all the BAD NEWS we hear today—from the media to the government sector—for us to survive these evil times, we must all put our hope and confidence in GOD through our PRAYER communication channel. *"Trust in him at all times; ye people, pour out your heart before him..."* (Psalms 62:8) In my opinion, no man can help you—especially when you do not know GOD. We must all develop a prayer lifestyle and put all our HOPE and EXPECTATION in GOD. *"My soul, wait thou only upon God; for my expectation is from him."* (Psalms 62:5) *"Confidence in an unfaithful man in time of trouble is like a broken tooth, and a foot out of joint."* (Proverbs 25:19)

2) WE COMMUNICATE OUR EXPECTATIONS THROUGH PRAYERS

It is written: *"Therefore I say unto you, what things soever ye desire, when ye pray, believe that ye receive them, and ye shall have them."* (Mark 11:24) We must communicate all our expectations to GOD.

In my opinion, whatever you do not have right now means you have not really been desperate about it. Unless we place a higher premium and make a desperate demand, GOD is not committed to intervene in our affairs. Every time we depend on GOD, we must cancel all alternatives. It is written: *"Give us help from trouble: for vain is the help of man."* (Psalms 108:12)

3) PRAYER HELPS MAKE US BETTER MORAL CITIZENS

A LIFESTYLE OF PRAYER makes us a better MORAL CITIZEN. It is written: *"All that the Father giveth me shall come to me; and him that cometh to me I will in no wise cast out."* (John 6:37) Everyone with a PRAYER LIFESTYLE REVERES, HONORS, RESPECTS and FEARS the LORD JESUS.

REMEMBER...

It is written: *"Wherefore I give you to understand, that no man speaking by the Spirit of God calleth Jesus accursed: and that no man can say that Jesus is the Lord, but by the Holy Ghost."* (1 Corinthians 12:3)

4) PRAYER DELIVERS US FROM EVIL

One of the greatest benefits of prayer is DELIVERANCE FROM EVIL. Recall, *"He shall call upon me, and I will answer him: I will be with him in trouble; I will deliver him, and honour him."* (Psalms 91:15) It is written: *"And call upon me in the day of trouble: I will deliver thee, and thou shalt glorify me."* (Psalms 50:15)

5. PRAYER HEALS OUR BODY, SOUL & SPIRIT.

Prayer is MEDICINAL to our soul, spirit and body. It is the prayer of faith that heals the sick. It is written: *"And the prayer of faith shall save the sick."* (James 5:15) Prayer comforts our spirit man and grants us assurance and rest.

THE LIFESTYLE OF PRAYER IS A LASTING LEGACY FOR OUR CHILDREN'S CHILDREN TO EMULATE AND FOLLOW THROUGHOUT THEIR LIVES

The lifestyle of prayer is the greatest inheritance we can leave behind for our children and for our children's children. *"A good man leaveth an inheritance to his children's children."* (Proverbs 13:22) One great example is Jonathan Edwards, the Puritan Preacher from the 1700s. Edwards and his wife Sarah left a great Godly legacy for their 11 children, compared to Max Jukes, who was a drunkard and never prayed in his lifetime. At the beginning of the 20th century, American educator and pastor A.E. Winship decided to trace out the descendants of Jonathan Edwards almost 150 years after his death.

Winship's findings regarding Edwards were remarkable, astounding and undeniable—especially when compared to those of Max Jukes. Jukes' legacy became public when the family trees of 42 different men in the New York prison system were traced back to him. Jonathan Edwards' PRAYER LEGACY includes: 1 U.S. Vice-President, 3 U.S. Senators, 3 governors, 3 mayors, 13 college presidents, 30 judges, 65 professors, 80 public office holders, 100 lawyers and 100 missionaries. Max Jukes' descendants included: 7 murderers, 60 thieves, 50 women of debauchery, 130 other convicts, 310 paupers (with over 2,300 years lived in poorhouses), 400 descendants who were physically wrecked by indulgent living. It was estimated that Max Jukes' descendants cost the state more than $1.25 million. Clearly, a prayer lifestyle has a profound impact on the children of all Godly families who depend on GOD in PRAYERS.

SUMMARY OF CHAPTER 3

—We must all depend on GOD.

—We must develop a lifestyle of prayer.

—We must train up our children to know and relate to GOD.

—We must communicate our pressing and relevant matters to GOD in prayers.

HIS DESTINY WAS THE CROSS....

HIS PURPOSE WAS LOVE....

HIS REASON WAS YOU....

FAIL MEANS:

F--------FIRST

A------ATTEMPT

I--------IN

L-------LEARNING

Henry Ford once said, "Failure is only the opportunity more intelligently to begin again." Perhaps you failed previously—it does not mean that you will fail again. Jesus said to Peter: *"But I have prayed for thee, that thy faith fail not: and when thou art converted, strengthen thy brethren."* (Luke 22:32) I admonish you in the Lord to pray again and you will see a positive outcome out of that detrimental situation.

PRAYER POINTS OVERCOME TRIALS BY THE HELP OF THE HOLY SPIRIT

1) Father Lord, deliver me from this present trial, in the Name of Jesus.

2) Almighty Father, break me out of this present obscurity, in the Name of Jesus.

3) Holy Spirit, help me to overcome this trial, in Jesus Name.

4) Holy Spirit, speak to me, in the Name of Jesus.

5) Holy Spirit, minister to my subconscious spirit, in the Name of Jesus.

6) Fire of God, burn down every mountain of difficulty, in the Name of Jesus.

7) Holy Ghost, baptize me with your fire, in the Name of Jesus.

8) Holy Spirit, go before me and favor me in this present challenge, in the Name of Jesus.

9) Spirit of God, grant me liberty and freedom by the fire of the Holy Spirit, in the Name of Jesus.

10) Father Lord, intervene on my behalf, in the Name of Jesus.

11) Ancient of day, liberate me this season, in the Name of Jesus.

12) Immortal redeemer, bring me higher above these prevailing changes.

13) Lord God, turn this present obstacale into my miracle, in the Name of Jesus.

14) Fire of God, break down these obstacles for me, in the Name of Jesus.

15) Holy Spirit, favor me in, Jesus Name.

16) Holy Spirit. release me from this challenge, in the Name of Jesus.

17) Holy Spirit, become my compionion, in Jesus Name.

18) Holy Spirit, represent me in this matter.

19) Holy Spirit, elevant me beyond my own immagina-

tion, in the Name of Jesus.

20) Holy Spirit, do not allow my enemies to truimph over my life, in the Name of Jesus.

21) Fire of God, protect me, in the Name of Jesus.

22) Fire of God, destroy my enemies, in the Name of Jesus.

23) Fire of God, build a wall around me, in the Name of Jesus.

24) Fire of God, expose my enemies, in the Name of Jesus.

25) Fire of God, prove yourself, in the Name of Jesus.

26) Holy Spirit, represent me in jesus name.

27) Holy Spirit, release your boldnes into my life.

28) Holy Spirit, grant me signs and wonders.

29) Holy Spirit, make me a living wonder in my lifetime.

30) Holy Spirit, turn my life around, in the Name of Jesus.

31) Holy Spirit, I will not remain at this level, in the Name of Jesus.

32) Spirit of God, lift me higher, in the mighty Name of Jesus.

33) Angels of God, minister unto me, in the Name of Jesus.

34) Hand of God, separate me this season, in the Name of Jesus.

HEALING KEYS

1) Always carry a positive mindset, regardless of the prevailing circumstances.

2) Always tell yourself the truth before you lie about it.

3) If the truth be told, you are a branch of His blessings, the planting of the Lord.

4) Never confess that you are sick to the hearing of the member of your body.

5) Positive confession with faith yields positive results.

6) Every cures of man have no power to prevail over your life.

7) A merry heart is medicinal and health to your body.

8) Spiritual and emotional well-being is vital to happiness in life.

9) To avoid depression, never have regrets.

10) Never be anxious in life to avoid anxiety.

11) Always live today for today to be at peace with your spirit and with God.

12) You're unique because your challenges are tailored to you only.

13) The blessing always dominates the curses any day.

14) Decisions are the wheels of life.

15) We either ride into fame or into shame.

16) Daily exercise and some reading of the Bible gurantees good health.

17) Every day is God's day. No day created by God is a disapointment.

18) Stay away from sweet stuff—they are temporary.

19) Sugar is sweet to your taste, beware! It also contributes to diabetes.

20) A good prayer life gurantees longivity.

21) People that pray in tongues do not develop mental disease.

22) Always be positive in everything.

23) Always have a mentor in life that will oppose and fight the tormentor.

24) Always have someone in life to learn from.

25) Tell everybody what you plan to do and someone will help you do it.

26) Winners fight to the last.

27) Quitters never win in life.

28) Soul winners are heirs to the kingdom of god.

29) Soul winners never lack help.

30) Soul winners are cerified with divine help.

31) God is always looking for soul winners to bless.

32) Life is a warfare and not a funfare.

33) In life you fight for all you possess.

34) No man or woman was born rich.

35) In your lifetime do something positive to impact your world.

36) Take care of your life today—you don't have one to spare.

37) Take your life serious before the devil take you down.

38) Always be cheerful at all times.

39) Regardless of the prevailing circumstances around you, your life is in the hand of God.

40) God is the super surgeon that will spiritually-surgically heal you.

41) Always expect help from above and not from abroad.

42) Man will disappoint you, but god will appoint you.

43) The joy of the lord is always our strength.

44) Spiritual height is not measured in length or breath.

45) If you go deeper with God, you will see deeper.

46) Your next level in life is full of recognition.

47) Go to where you are celebrated and not where you are tolerated.

48) Develop yourself in the area of your calling in life.

49) A lifestyle of thanks given keeps God 24/7 on duty on our behalf.

50) Develop a lifestyle of thanksgiving.

51) Thanksgiving guarantees our access to obtain the promises.

DECISION KEYS

1) Nothing changes until you make up your mind.

2) Decision is the gateway to deliverance.

3) Until you decide, no one will decide for you.

4) Your prosperity is proportional to your decisions.

5) The decision you make will determine the future you will create

6) Decision creates future and fulfills destinies.

7) Decision beautifies our future.

8) Decision keeps you out of trouble.

9) Decision exempts you from evil.

10) Decision gurantees eternity.

11) You can only go far in life by your faith decisions.

12) You are poor because you made such decisions

13) Make a decision and change your life.

14) Life changing decisions are a function of quality information.

15) Success in life is a function of decision.

16) Life experiences are full of decisions.

17) Decisions change destinies.

18) Never settle for information—always look for revelation.

19) You are where you are today based on your last decision.

20) Information is crucial in decision making.

21) Decision makers rule the world.

22) You can rule your world with quality decisions.

23) As long as you decide rightly, Satan cannot harrass you.

IN SUMMARY

Is any among you afflicted? let him pray. Is any merry? let him sing psalms. Is any sick among you? let him call for the elders of the church; and let them pray over him, anointing him with oil in the name of the Lord: And the prayer of faith shall save the sick, and the Lord shall raise him up; and if he have committed sins, they shall be forgiven him. Confess your faults one to another, and pray one for another, that ye may be healed. The effectual fervent prayer of a righteous man availeth much. with the Holy Ghost and with power: who went about doing good, and healing all that were oppressed of the devil; for God was with him.
James 5:13-16

CONCLUSION

And it came to pass about an eight days after these sayings, he took Peter and John and James, and went up into a mountain to pray. And as he prayed, the fashion of his countenance was altered, and his raiment was white and glistering.
Luke 9:28-29

JOHN WESLEY, who started the METHODIST CHURCH, once said "IT APPEARS LIKE GOD WILL DO NOTHING UNTIL SOMEBODY PRAYS."

Although in the physical realm we deal with challenges, physical shortcomings and obstacles, we'll keep going through trials and tribulations unless we DOMINATE in the REALMS of the SPIRIT by PRAYING. We will never emerge victorious in our life time until we do so. Many years ago, the Queen of England said, "I fear nothing but the prayers of JOHN KNOX," who was a man of PRAYER from Scotland.

For Herod feared John, knowing that he was a just man and an holy, and observed him; and when he heard him, he did many things, and heard him gladly.
Mark 6:20

King Herold FEARED JOHN THE BAPTIST because JOHN was a righteous MAN OF PRAYER. We must all incorporate PRAYERS into our lives, THE LIFESTYLE OF PRAYER. The only channel to get GOD involved in our daily trials and challenges is by PRAYING UNTO GOD. *"I will not leave you comfortless: I will come to you. But the Comforter, which is the Holy Ghost, whom the Father will send in my name, he shall teach you all things, and bring all things to your remembrance, whatsoever I have said unto you."* (John 14:26) We must therefore develop a lifestyle of praying often to GOD. "And he spake a parable unto them to this end, that men ought always to pray, and not to faint." (Luke 18:1) My book, *The Lifestyle of Prayers*, will help ENERGIZE YOUR PRAYER LIFE.

CHAPTER 4
PRAYER OF SALVATION

Neither is there salvation in any other: for there is none other name under heaven given among men, whereby we must be saved.
Acts 4:12

Now we know that God heareth not sinners: but if any man be a worshipper of God, and doeth his will, him he heareth.
John 9:31

We must therefore be joined with Christ.....

Therefore if any man be in Christ, he is a new creature: old things are passed away; behold, all things are become new.
2 Corinthians 5:17

Now repeat this Prayer after me.

Say Lord Jesus, I accept you today, as my Lord and my savior. Forgive me of my sins, wash me with your blood. Right now, I believe I am sanctified, I am saved, I am free. I am free from the power of sin, to serve the Lord Jesus. Thank you Lord for saving me. Amen.

Congratulations. You are now...

A BORN AGAIN CHRISTIAN.

Again I say to you—CONGRATULATIONS!

What must I do to BE SAVED?

To BE SAVED, YOU MUST BE BORN AGAIN!

The word says as many as received him, to them gave He power to become the sons of God. Even to them that believe on his name.

To qualify for SALVATION, do the following sincerely:

1) Acknowledge that you are a sinner and that He died for you. (Romans 3:23)

2) Repent of your sins. (Acts 3:19, Luke 13:5, 2 Peter 3:9)

3) Believe in your heart that Jesus died for your sin. (Romans 10:10)

4) Confess Jesus as the Lord over your life. (Romans 10:10, Acts 2:21)

Now repeat this Prayer after me:

Say Lord Jesus, I accept you today, as my Lord and my savior, forgive me of my sins wash me with your blood. Right now, I believe, I am sanctified, I am save, I am free, I am free from the Power of sin to serve the Lord Jesus.
Thank you Lord for saving me.
Amen.

Congratulations—

YOU ARE NOW A BORN AGAIN CHRISTIAN!

AGAIN I SAY TO YOU CONGRATULATIONS

I adjure you to watch the Spirit of God bear witness with your Spirit confirming His word with signs following. The word says The Spirit itself beareth witness with our spirit, that we are the children of God. Join a Bible-believing church, or join us on our weekly and Sunday worship services at 343 Sanford Avenue Newark, New Jersey 07106.

HEALING KEYS

1) Always carry a positive mindset, regardless of the prevailing circumstances.

2) Always tell yourself the truth before you lie about it.

3) If the truth be told, you are a branch of His blessings, the planting of the Lord.

4) Never confess that you are sick to the hearing of the member of your body.

5) Positive confession with faith yields positive results.

6) Every cures of man have no power to prevail over your life.

7) A merry heart is medicinal and health to your body.

8) Spiritual and emotional well-being is vital to happiness in life.

9) To avoid depression, never have regrets.

10) Never be anxious in life to avoid anxiety.

11) Always live today for today to be at peace with your spirit and with God.

12) You're unique because your challenges are tailored to you only.

13) The blessing always dominates the curses any day.

14) Decisions are the wheels of life.

15) We either ride into fame or into shame.

16) Daily exercise and some reading of the Bible gurantees good health.

17) Every day is God's day. No day created by God is a disapointment.

18) Stay away from sweet stuff—they are temporary.

19) Sugar is sweet to your taste, beware! It also contributes to diabetes.

20) A good prayer life gurantees longivity.

21) People that pray in tongues do not develop mental disease.

22) Always be positive in everything.

23) Always have a mentor in life that will oppose and fight the tormentor.

24) Always have someone in life to learn from.

25) Tell everybody what you plan to do and someone will help you do it.

26) Winners fight to the last.

27) Quitters never win in life.

28) Soul winners are heirs to the kingdom of god.

29) Soul winners never lack help.

30) Soul winners are cerified with divine help.

31) God is always looking for soul winners to bless.

32) Life is a warfare and not a funfare.

33) In life you fight for all you possess.

34) No man or woman was born rich.

35) In your lifetime do something positive to impact your world.

36) Take care of your life today—you don't have one to spare.

37) Take your life serious before the devil take you down.

38) Always be cheerful at all times.

39) Regardless of the prevailing circumstances around you, your life is in the hand of God.

40) God is the super surgeon that will spiritually-surgically heal you.

41) Always expect help from above and not from abroad.

42) Man will disappoint you, but god will appoint you.

43) The joy of the lord is always our strength.

44) Spiritual height is not measured in length or breath.

45) If you go deeper with God, you will see deeper.

46) Your next level in life is full of recognition.

47) Go to where you are celebrated and not where you are tolerated.

48) Develop yourself in the area of your calling in life.

49) A lifestyle of thanks given keeps God 24/7 on duty on our behalf.

50) Develop a lifestyle of thanksgiving.

51) Thanksgiving guarantees our access to obtain the promises.

WISDOM KEYS

— Every productive society is a society heading to the top.

—Millions of Nigerians run away from Nigeria. Very few Nigerians stay in Nigeria.

—My decision to return Nigeria is the will of God for my life.

—My shortcoming in America after 18 years is the fact that I've trained me to be wise, to think, reflect and reason appropriately.

—If you train your mind to reason, it will train your hands to earn money.

—It is absurd to use the money of the heathen to build the kingdom of the living God.

—Every ministry reveals its agenda and VISION either at the beginning or at the end.

—Be careful of your life. It is your first ministry.

—The average American mind is conditioned for a continual quest to get new things and discard the old.

—When I considered well, my BMW jeep became my initial deposit for the work of the ministry in Nigeria.

—Money will never fall from any tree or person. Make up your mind to be independent today.

—Everyone is waiting for you to change your mind. Until you change your thinking, nothing changes around you.

—Multiple academic degrees in other disciplines gave me the chance to think and reason.

—Whatever anyone is thinking at any time reveals what is inside of their heart.

—All planned events are the product of meditation.

—Every event is designed for a designated timeline.

—Wisdom is your ability to think, to create and invent.

— If you can think wisely enough, you will come out of debt.

—The distance between you and your success is your innovative and creative ability to think well.

—Success is the result of hard work, commitment, resolve and determined learning from past mistakes and failings.

—If you organize your mind, you have organized your

life and destiny.

—There is a thin line between success and failure.

—Wealth is your ability to think, power is your ability to reason and success is your ability to be informed.

—If you can make use of your mind by thinking and reasoning, God will make use of your life and destiny.

—Reflect, reason, think and be Great.

—Famous people are born of woman.

—That you will make it is your intention, that you will survive is your resolve, that you will succeed with changes is your determination, personal efforts and hard work.

—No man was born a failure.

—Lack of vision is the result of failure.

—Working with mental patients encourages and aspire me to be a productive observant and dedicated to my assignment.

—Successful people are not magicians. It is the will-power, combined with hard work and determination and a resolve to succeed, that make them succeed.

—In the unequivocal state of the mind, intention is not a location or a position. It is the state of the mind.

—So many people think that they think.

—The mind is used to think, to reflect and to reason.

—You will remain blind with your eyes open until you can see with your mind by thinking.

—There is no favoritism in accurate and precise calculation.

—Although knowledge is power, information is the key and gateway to a great future.

—It will take the hand of God to move the hand of man.

—With the backing of the great wise God, nothing will disconnect you from your inheritance.

—As long as you have wisdom and understanding of God, Satan and evil cannot manipulate your life and destiny.

—You have come this far in life by your own judgment and the decisions you made in the past. Now lean in and listen to God for another dimension of greatness.

—Great people are ordinary people. It is extra ordinary efforts and the price of sacrifice that produces greatness in them.

—As a mental direct care worker, I saw a great pastor and a motivational speaker within myself.

—A menial job does not reduce your self-worth. Until you resolve to achieve greatness and see greatness in all you do, you will never count in your community.

—The principle of Jesus will solve your gambling and addiction problems.

—The man of Jesus will lead you into heaven.

—Everyone has their self-appraisal and what they think about you. Until you discover yourself, other opinions about you will alter the real you.

—Supervisors and directors are just a position in the chain of command in a workplace. Never allow your supervisor hierarchy to alter your opinion of yourself.

—Everyone can come out of debt if they make up their mind.

—The fact that I am not a decision-maker at work does not diminish my contribution to my world.

—Although it appears like it was a poor decision to accept a direct care employment at a psychiatric hospital, as I reflect on my nine years of that experience, it became apparent that I have learned and experienced enough for my next assignment.

—Self-encouragement and determination is a resolve of the heart.

—If you are determined to make a difference and do the things that make a difference, you will eventually make a difference.

—Good things do not come easy.

—Short cuts will cut your life short.

—Those who look ahead move ahead.

—Life is all about making an impact. In your lifetime strive to make an impact in your community.

—Make friends and connect with people who are moving ahead of you in life.

—If you can look around well, you have come a long way in your life, made a lot of difference and realized a lot of success in life.

—If you are my old friend, hurry up to reach out to me

before I become a stranger to you.

—I am blessed with inspirations from God that changed my interpretation of the world around me.

—I thought I was stagnant and lonely until I looked around and noticed my children running around and my wife cooking.

—At 40, I resigned my job to seek the Lord forever.

—My ministry took a drastic rise to the top when the wisdom of God visited me with knowledge and understanding.

—You will be a better person if you understand the characteristics of your personality like your mood swings, attitudes and habits.

—It is the seed of love you sow into the heart of a child and a woman that you reap in due time.

—Love is not selfish. Love shares everything, including the concealed secrets of the mind.

—As long as you have a prayer life and a Bible, you will never feel lonely in the race of life.

—When good friends disconnect from you, let them go. They might have seen something new in a different direction.

—Confidence in yourself and in God is the only way to bring you out of captivity

—Never train a child to waste his or her time.

—The mind is the greatest asset of a great future.

—You walk by common sense, run by principles and fly by instruction.

—Those who become successful in life did it by self-determination, hard work and learning from past failures.

—Most successful people are lonely people. No one renders help to them, believing they are already successful. Except when they seek for more knowledge and information, they are all alone.

— I have seen a towing truck vehicle. I have also seen a towing ship in the water. But I have never seen a towing airplane in the air.

—I exercise my judgment and make a decision every minute of the day. Decisions are crucial, critical and vital with reference to your future.

—So many people wish for a great future. You can only work towards a great future.

—Your celebrity status began when you discovered your talent. What are you good at? Work at it with all your commitment.

—Prayers will sustain you, but the wisdom of God will prosper you.

—When I met Oyedepo, his teachings changed my perspective. But when I met Ibiyeomie, his teachings changed my perception.

— I will be successful in ministry if only I concentrate and focus my energy in the work of the ministry.

— It took the late Dr. Norman Vincent Peale's book to open my mind towards the kingdom of success.

PRAYER OF SALVATION

I am glad you have read this book all the way from the beginning to this point. All I have said from the beginning will remain a mystery until you commit it into practice.

And before you do so, I want you—if you have not given your life to Jesus already—to do so now. Give your life to Christ. I want you to know the truth! The truth is that Jesus died for your sins and because He died, you must be alive and prosperous.

What must I do to determine my divine visitation?

To determine divine visitation, you must be born again! The word says, *"As many as received Him, to them gave He power to become the sons of God. Even to them that believe on his name."* (John 1:12)

To qualify for divine visitation, do the following with sincerity—

> 1) Acknowledge that you are a sinner and that He died for you. (Romans 3:23)
> 2) Repent of your sins. (Acts 3:19, Luke 13:5, 2 Peter 3:9)
> 3) Believe in your heart that Jesus died for your sins. (Romans 10:10)
> 4) Confess Jesus as the Lord over your life. (Romans 10:10, Acts 2:21)

Now repeat this prayer after me:

Say Lord Jesus, I accept you today, as my Lord and my savior. Forgive me of my sins, wash me with your blood. Right now, I believe I am sanctified, I am saved, I am free. I am free from the power of sin, to serve the Lord Jesus. Thank you Lord for saving me. Amen.

Congratulations. You are now...

A BORN AGAIN CHRISTIAN.

Again I say to you—CONGRATULATIONS!

I adjure you to watch the Spirit of God bear witness with your Spirit, confirming His word with subsequent signs. The word says, *"The Spirit itself beareth witness with our spirit, that we are the children of God."*

MIRACLE CARE OUTREACH

"...But that the members should have the same care one for another"
1 Corinthians 12:25

We are all members of the body of Christ. Jesus commanded us to love our neighbor as ourselves. This includes caring for one another as a member of one body. True love is expressed in caring and giving. The word says, for God so Love He gave....

Reach out to someone in need of Jesus. Help someone in crisis find Christ. Look out and prove your love to Jesus by caring and inviting your friends and associates to find Jesus the Healer.

Invite your friends to our Home Care Cell Fellowship (Miracle Chapel Intl. Satellite Fellowship). We're in the U.S. at 33 Schley Street, Newark, New Jersey 07112. Home Care Cell Fellowship Group meets every Tuesday at 6:00pm-7:00pm.

If you are in Nigeria—MIRACLE OF GOD MINISTRIES, aka "MIRACLE CHAPEL INTL." Mpama–Egbu-Owerri Imo state Nigeria.

LIFE IS NOT ALL ABOUT DURATION, BUT IT'S ALL ABOUT DONATION

What does this statement mean?
Life consists not in accumulation of material

wealth. (Luke 12:15) But it's all about liberality...i.e., what you can give and share with others. (Proverbs 11:25) When you live for others, you live forever—because you outlive your generation by the legacy you leave behind after you depart into glory to be with the Lord. But when you live for yourself, when you are reduced to SELF—you are easily forgotten when you die and depart in glory.

Permit me to admonish you today to live your life to be a blessing to a soul connected to you today. I want you to know that so many souls are connected and looking up to you, and through you so many souls will be saved and rescued from destruction. Will you disciple someone today to find Jesus Christ?

As a genuine Christian, it is your duty to evangelize Jesus Christ to all you meet on your way. Jesus is still in the healing business—Jesus is still doing miracles, from time of old to now. Therefore, tell someone about Jesus Christ today, disciple and bring them to Church. *Philip findeth Nathanael...* (John 1:45)

Please prove the sincerity of your love for God today, please become a soul winner. The dignity of your Christianity is hidden in your boldness to proclaim and evangelize Jesus Christ to all you meet on your way. There is a question mark on the integrity of your Christianity until you become a life soul winner. Invite someone to join us worship the Lord Jesus this coming Sunday. Amen.

MIRACLE OF GOD MINISTRIES
PILLARS OF THE COMMISSION

We Believe, Preach and Practice the following:

1) We believe and preach Salvation to every living human being.

2) We believe and preach Repentance and Forgiveness of sins.

3) We believe and preach the baptism of the Holy Spirit and Spiritual gifts.

4) We believe and teach Prosperity.

5) We believe and preach Divine Healing and Miracles—Signs and Wonder.

6) We believe and preach Faith.

7) We believe and proclaim the Power of God (Supernatural).

8) We believe and proclaim Praise and Worship to God.

9) We believe and preach Wisdom.

10) We believe and preach Holiness (Consecration).

11) We believe and preach Vision.

12) We believe and teach the Word of God.

13) We believe and teach Success.

14) We believe and practice Prayer.

15) We believe and teach Deliverance.

These 15 stones form the Pillars of Our Commission. Become part of this church family and follow this great move of God.

MY HEARTFELT PRAYER FOR YOU

It is my burning desire for God to touch you through one of our teaching books or CDs. It also my personal desire for you encounter God for yourself.

Now let me Pray for you:

OH GOD, YOUR PRECIOUS SON/DAUGHTER HAS COME IN AGREEMENT TO SEEK FOR HELP FROM THEE. I PRAY, BY THE INTERCESSION OF THE HOLY SPIRIT LET THERE BE REWARDS FOR ALL OUR PRAYERS IN THE MIGHT NAME OF JESUS. AMEN.

THE REWARD OF PRAYERS

For all our prayers, supplication and intercession to be rewarded, we must ask in faith. *"Ye ask, and receive not, because ye ask amiss, that ye may consume it upon your lusts."* (James 4:3)

As men and women of prayer, we must repent from every unrighteousness. *"The sacrifices of God are a broken spirit: a broken and a contrite heart, O God, thou wilt not despise."* (Psalms 51:17)

BEWARE!! BE WARNED !! BE CAREFUL!!

> *Nevertheless, the foundation of God standeth sure, having this seal, The Lord knoweth them that are his. And, let every one that nameth the name of Christ depart from iniquity. But in a great house there are not only vessels of gold and of silver, but also of wood and of earth; and some to honour, and some to dishonour. If a man therefore purge himself from these, he shall be a vessel unto honour, sanctified, and meet for the master's use, and prepared unto every good work.*
> **2 Timothy 2:19-21**

AS YOU REPENT, I SEE GOD MOVING IN A NEW DIMENSION OF A HIGHER ODER. I SEE GOD BREAKING DOWN BARRIERS FOR YOU. I SEE GOD BRINGING DELIVERANCE INTO YOUR FAMILY.

WE MUST MAKE PLANS FOR ETERNITY

We must make up our minds to make heaven at last. HEAVEN IS REAL AND HELL IS CERTAIN.

Where do YOU intend to go?

I love you so much that I want to see you make heaven at last. We must tell everyone about Jesus Christ. We must win souls for the kingdom of God.

ABOUT THE AUTHOR

Rev. Franklin N. Abazie is the founding and Presiding Pastor of Miracle of God Ministries, with headquarters in Newark, New Jersey USA and a branch church in Owerri-Imo State Nigeria. He is following the footsteps of one of his mentors, the healing evangelist Oral Roberts of the blessed memory. The Lord passed Oral Roberts' healing mantle two days before he went to be with the Lord at age 91 into the hands of healing evangelist Rev. Franklin N. Abazie in a vision.

In all his services, the Power and Presence of God is present to heal all in his audience. Rev. Abazie is an ordained man of God, with a Healing Ministry reviving the healing and miracle ministry of Jesus Christ of Nazareth.

Pastor Franklin N. Abazie, has been called by God with a unique mandate: **"THE MOMENT IS DUE TO IMPACT YOUR WORLD THROUGH THE REVIVAL OF THE HEALING AND MIRACLE MINISTRY OF JESUS CHRIST OF NAZARETH.**

"I AM SENDING YOU TO RESTORE HEALTH UNTO THEE AND I WILL HEAL THEE OF THY WOUNDS, SAID THE LORD OF HOST."

Rev. Abazie is a gifted, ardent teacher of the word of God, who operates also in the office of a

Prophet, generating and attracting undeniable signs and wonders, special miracles and healings, with apostolic fireworks of the Holy Ghost. He is the founding and presiding senior Pastor of this fast growing Healing Ministry. He has written over 86 inspirational, healing and transforming books covering almost all aspects of divine healing and life. He is happily married and blessed with children.

BOOKS BY REV. FRANKLIN N. ABAZIE:

1) The Outcome of Faith
2) Understanding the Secret of Prevailing Prayers
3) Commanding Abundance
4) Understanding the Secret of the Man God Uses
5) Activating My Due Season
6) Overcoming Divine Verdicts
7) The Outcome of Divine Wisdom
8) Understanding God's Restoration Mandate
9) Walking In the Victory and Authority of the Truth
10) God's Covenant Exemption
11) Destiny Restoration Pillars
12) Provoking Acceptable Praise
13) Understanding Divine Judgment
14) Activating Angelic Re-enforcement
15) Provoking Un-Merited Favo
16) The Benefits of the Speaking Faith
17) Understanding Divine Arrangement
18) How to Keep Your Healing
19) Understanding the Mysteries of the Speaking Faith
20) Understanding the Mysteries of Prophetic Healing
21) Operating Under the Rules of Creative Healing
22) Understanding the Joy of Breakthrough
23) Understanding the Mystery of Breakthrough
24) Understanding Divine Prosperity
25) Understanding Divine Healing
26) Retaining Your Inheritance
27) Overcoming Confusing Spirit
28) Commanding Angelic Escorts

29) Enforcing Your Inheritance In Christ Jesus
30) Understanding Your Guardian Angels
31) Overcoming the Dominion of Sin
32) Understanding the Voice of God
33) The Outstanding Benefits of the Anointing
34) The Audacity of the Blood of Jesus
35) Walking in the Reality of the Anointing
36) Escaping the Nightmare of Poverty
37) Understanding Your Harvest Season
38) Activating Your Success Buttons
39) Overcoming the Forces of Darkness
40) Overcoming the Devices of the Devil
41) Overcoming Demonic Agents
42) Overcoming the Sorrows of Failure
43) Rejecting the Sorrows of Failure
44) Resisting the Sorrows of Poverty
45) Restoring Broken Marriages
46) Redeeming Your Days
47) The Force of Vision
48) Overcoming the Forces of Ignorance
49) Understanding the Sacrifice of Small Beginning
50) The Might of Small Beginning
51) Understanding the Mysteries of Prophesy
52) Overcoming Dream Nightmares
53) Breaking the Shackles of the Curse of the Law
54) Understanding the Joy of Harvest
55) Wisdom for Signs & Wonders
56) Wisdom for Generational Impact
57) Wisdom for Marriage Stability
58) Understanding the Number of Your Days

59) Enforcing Your Kingdom Rights
60) Escaping the Traps of Immoralities
61) Escaping the Trap of Poverty
62) Accessing Biblical Prosperity
63) Accessing True Riches in Christ
64) Silencing the Voice of the Accuser
65) Overcoming the Forces of Oppositions
66) Quenching the Voice of the Avenger
67) Silencing Demonic Prediction & Projection
68) Silencing Your Mocker
69) Understanding the Power of the Holy Ghost
70) Understanding the Baptism of Power
71) The Mystery of the Blood of Jesus
72) Understanding the Mystery of Sanctification
73) Understanding the Power of Holiness
74) Understanding the Forces of Purity & Righteousness
75) Activating the Forces of Vengeance
76) Appreciating the Mystery of Restoration
77) Overcoming the Projection & Prediction of the Enemy
78) Engaging the Mystery of the Blood
79) Commanding the Power of the Speaking Faith
80) Uprooting the Forces Against Your Rising
81) Overcoming Mere Success Syndrome
82) Understanding Divine Sentence
83) Understanding the Mystery of Praise
84) Understanding the Author of Faith
85) The Mystery of the Finisher of Faith
86) Attracting Supernatural Favor

MIRACLE OF GOD MINISTRIES
NIGERIA CRUSADE
2012

MIRACLE OF GOD MINISTRIES
NIGERIA CRUSADE 2012

MIRACLE OF GOD MINISTRIES

NIGERIA CRUSADE

2012

MIRACLE OF GOD MINISTRIES

NIGERIA CRUSADE

2012

MIRACLE OF GOD MINISTRIES

NIGERIA CRUSADE 2012

www.ingramcontent.com/pod-product-compliance
Lightning Source LLC
Chambersburg PA
CBHW021445080526
44588CB00009B/702